CHIP INGRAM

THE INVISIBLE WAR

WHAT EVERY BELIEVER NEEDS TO KNOW ABOUT SATAN, DEMONS, and SPIRITUAL WARFARE

Introduction

Some people may say, "Come on, Chip, do you really believe there's some kind of invisible war lurking beneath our tangible landscape?"

My answer: *"I know there is."*

The Bible clearly teaches us that Satan is on a mission to destroy God's people. And the problem is, Satan doesn't telegraph his temptations and schemes. Instead, he's very secretive as he attempts to lead Christians down a delicate, subtle, gradual path of deception.

C.S. Lewis wrote: "Indeed, the safest road to hell is the gradual one — the gentle slope, soft underfoot, without sudden turns, without milestones, without signposts."

Satan wants to get an unnoticeable foothold in our lives by triggering relational conflicts; weighing us down with fear, anxiety, depression, or insecurity; increasing our selfishness; tempting us with escape mechanisms such as drugs and alcohol; and seducing us through the lust of the eyes, lust of the flesh, and boastful pride of life.

So, you may ask, "If there is an unseen battle, how can I defend myself? How can I win?" That's what we're about to study in this new eight-part series entitled The Invisible War. Let's open our Bibles up and see what God has to say about Satan's goals and tactics, the spiritual armor God offers us, and the confidence we can have about our sure victory over the Enemy. May this study increase your wisdom and strengthen you for the future!

Keep pressin' ahead,

Chip Ingram
Teaching Pastor, Living on the Edge

WHAT IS THE INVISIBLE WAR?

Ephesians 6:10—12

What Is The Invisible War?

Our imagination flirts with the "unseen world." On a night of channel surfing we may see how a medium helps police solve crimes, or witness an "exorcism" on a news magazine.

What if we could pull back that curtain and peer into that world? What would it look like?

- *Are there angels? Are there demons?*

- *Does Satan exist or is he a children's caricature brandishing a pitchfork?*

- *Can someone be possessed by a demon?*

- *Is there an unseen battle being waged around me?*

- *If there is an unseen battle, how can I defend myself?*

Chip kicks off this series with a call to remove the blinders and gaze into the unseen world. Perhaps we will see what we do not see: the invisible war.

VIDEO NOTES

[10]Finally, be strong in the Lord and in the strength of His might. [11]Put on the full armor of God, so that you will be able to stand firm against the schemes of the devil. [12]For our struggle is not against flesh and blood, but against the rulers, against the powers, against the world forces of this darkness, against the spiritual forces of wickedness in the heavenly places.

Ephesians 6:10—12 (NASB)

I. _____ **Command** *Verse 10*

"Allow yourself to be continually strengthened by the power already made available to you in your new position and relationship with Christ." It is the power that raised Christ from the dead and now dwells in you.

II. _____ **Command** *Verse 11*

How? By continually and repeatedly putting on, at specific points in time, the spiritual protection God has provided for you...for the express purpose of holding on to your position in Christ as you are bombarded by Satanic schemes designed to destroy you and/or render you ineffective in Kingdom pursuits.

III. The _____ **for Commands in Verses 10–11** *Verse 12*

It's because our real struggle (battle, wrestling match to the death) is not against physical/material adversaries (people, circumstances, organizations), but against a hierarchy of demonic forces doing battle in the spiritual realm.

Basic Truths About Spiritual Warfare

1. There is an invisible world that is just as _____ as the Visible World. — *Ephesians 6:12*

2. We are involved in an _____ war, a cosmic conflict that has eternal implications. — *Ephesians 6:12*

³For though we walk in the flesh, we do not war according to the flesh, ⁴for the weapons of our warfare are not of the flesh, but divinely powerful for the destruction of fortresses. ⁵We are destroying speculations and every lofty thing raised up against the knowledge of God, and we are taking every thought captive to the obedience of Christ,...

2 Corinthians 10:3—5 (NASB)

...in whose case the god of this world has blinded the minds of the unbelieving, that they might not see the light of the gospel of the glory of Christ, who is the image of God.

2 Corinthians 4:4 (NASB)

DISCUSSION QUESTIONS

1. When you hear the phrase, "spiritual warfare" what immediately comes to your mind? After watching today's teaching, how has your perspective of spiritual warfare changed?

_____

_____

_____

2. What is your reaction to people when they attribute their problems to demonic activity?

3. Are there times when you consider their explanations valid? Are there times when you dismiss them right away? What makes the difference?

4. What is your natural tendency in conflict — to fight or flee? Does this tendency undermine God's strength in your life? If so, how?

5. Have you ever considered that a besetting sin or an unresolved conflict could in any way be related to spiritual warfare?

Session 1 Keys

We are commanded to engage in an invisible war.

The unseen world is just as real as the visible one.

ACTION STEPS

Think about Chip's question from the video, "When was the last time you honestly considered that some struggle or relational conflict was rooted in satanic opposition?"

In most struggles, we are quick to blame ourselves, others, or societal problems. Spend time in prayer – ask God to give you greater awareness.

Be more observant this week of the invisible battle.

AT HOME

Philip Yancy describes how little we truly "see" compared to animals:

"Every animal on earth has a set of correspondences with the environment around it, and some of those correspondences far exceed ours. Humans can perceive only thirty percent of the range of the sun's light and 1/70th of the spectrum of electromagnetic energy. Many animals exceed our abilities. Bats detect insects by sonar; pigeons navigate by magnetic fields; bloodhounds perceive a world of smell unavailable to us."

Have you ever thought about our limitations when it comes to the spiritual realms? If the apostle Paul commands us to enter in "spiritual warfare," what are some ways you can increase your sensitivity to this invisible war?

MEMORY VERSE

Finally, be strong in the Lord, and in the strength of His might. Put on the full armor of God, that you may be able to stand firm against the schemes of the devil.

Ephesians 6:10—11 (NASB)

WHO ARE WE FIGHTING?

Ephesians 6:10—12

Who Are We Fighting?

Picture this. It's Super Bowl Sunday. Both teams are ready. They have dreamed about this game all season. But for the last two weeks they've done a lot more than dream — they have watched hour after hour of film.

What gives them more hope than the teams that were eliminated weeks ago? They know the opposition and have learned their schemes. There will be no surprises because they've done the math. Why? Because they want to win.

Fortunately our Enemy's plans have fallen into our hands — not by accident, but by intention. Tucked inside the folds of our Bibles, God details how we can resist his predictable ploys, his cunning deceptions, and his sinister schemes.

VIDEO NOTES

Five Basic Truths About Spiritual Warfare (cont'd)

1. There is an invisible world that is just as real as the visible world.

2. We are involved in an invisible war, a cosmic conflict that has eternal implications.

3. Our foe is _____ and His goal is to destroy us and discredit the cause of Christ. — *Ephesians 6:12*

Be of sober spirit, be on the alert. Your adversary, the devil, prowls about like a roaring lion, seeking someone to devour.

1 Peter 5:8 (NASB)

But Michael, the archangel, when he disputed with the devil and argued about the body of Moses, did not dare pronounce against him a railing judgment, but said, "The Lord rebuke you."

Jude 1:9 (NASB)

4. We must respect our foe, but not fear him — become acutely _____ of his "methods," but not be preoccupied by them. — *Ephesians 6:11*

Paul agrees to forgive a brother along with the Corinthian church... "so that no advantage would be taken of us by Satan; for we are not ignorant of his schemes."

2 Corinthians 2:11 (NASB)

Satan's names reveal his _____ .

Satan attacks _____ _____ , the church, by...

- False philosophies (Colossians 2:8)
- False religions (1 Corinthians 10:19)
- False ministers (2 Corinthians 11:14–15)
- False doctrine (1 John 2:18)
- False disciples (Matthew 13)
- False morals (2 Thessalonians 2:7)

Satan attacks _____ _____ by...

- Deceiving men (2 Corinthians 4:4)
- Destroying life (Hebrews 2:14)
- Persecuting the saints (Revelation 2:10)
- Preventing service (1 Thessalonians 2:18)
- Promoting schisms (2 Corinthians 2:10, 11)
- Planting doubt (Genesis 3:1–2)
- Provoking sin
- Producing sects/cults (1 Timothy 4:1)

Satan's power is _____ .

- He is created, therefore not omniscient or infinite
- He can be resisted by the Christian (James 4:7)
- God places limitations on him (Job 1:12)

5. As believers in Christ, we do not fight "for" victory, we fight "from" victory. In Christ's power we are invincible! — Ephesians 6:10

Promises From God Concerning Victory Over Satan:

You are from God, little children, and have overcome them; because greater is He who is in you than he who is in the world.

1 John 4:4 (NASB)

⁴For whatever is born of God overcomes the world; and this is the victory that has overcome the world — our faith. ⁵And who is the one who overcomes the world, but he who believes that Jesus is the Son of God?

1 John 5:4—5 (NASB)

And they overcame him because of the blood of the Lamb and because of the word of their testimony, and they did not love their life even to death.

Revelation 12:11 (NASB)

Submit therefore to God. Resist the devil and he will flee from you.

James 4:7 (NASB)

DISCUSSION QUESTIONS

1. Someone once said, "The best crime Satan ever perpetrated was to convince the world he did not exist." Do you agree? Why or why not?

2. Prior to today's teaching, if someone asked you to describe Satan and where he came from, what would you have said? How has your perspective changed?

3. We learned in today's teaching that Satan attacks God's people and God's program. Quickly review the ways that Satan attacks God's people and share with the group which area you believe you're most prone to attack and why.

4. In like manner, examine the long list of ways that Satan attacks God's program, the Church, and share one or two new insights that you gained about Satan's tactics against God's program.

5. Of the four promises from God over Satan, which one gave you the most hope and why?

_____

_____

_____

Session 2 Keys

Satan is a real and dangerous foe. Satan is a limited being. For the believer, God assures victory over Satan.

ACTION STEPS

Chip spoke of the need for "balance" in our assessment of spiritual opposition.

1. On a scale of one to ten (one being too little and ten being too much), how much credit have you given to the reality of demonic activity in your life? Why?

_____

_____

_____

2. What has been Satan's game plan to defeat you?

_____

_____

The devil is a better theologian than any of us and is a devil still.

A. W Tozer

AT HOME

Look below at Isaiah 14:12–14:

> ¹²*How you are fallen from heaven, O Day Star, son of Dawn! How you are cut down to the ground, you who laid the nations low!* ¹³*You said in your heart, 'I will ascend to heaven; above the stars of God I will set my throne on high; I will sit on the mount of assembly in the far reaches of the north;* ¹⁴*I will ascend above the heights of the clouds; I will make myself like the Most High.*

Isaiah 14:12—14 (ESV)

Underline the words, "I will," every time they are used. Satan fell because, though he was created as the highest of all angels, he had his eyes on what he didn't have. How many times do you catch yourself saying, "If I only had _____ I would be happy." Satan's tactics haven't changed since the Garden.

1. *What specific phrases flash in your mind? List them:*

_____

_____

_____

2. *Counter them with how God has blessed your life. List them:*

_____

_____

_____

Every time those phrases flash in your mind, counter them by remembering God's blessings in your life.

MEMORY VERSE

You are from God, little children, and have overcome them; because greater is He who is in you than he who is in the world.

I John 4:4 (NASB)

FOUR KEYS TO
SPIRITUAL
VICTORY

Ephesians 6:13–15

Four Keys To Spiritual Victory

Have you ever sat on the runway for what appears to be an eternity as they "de-ice" the plane? Any pilot will tell you that just 1/8 an inch of ice coating the wings can cause a crash.

It proves that just a little bit will hurt.

Satan rarely tempts us with the "big sins." Few of us wake up one morning with the thought, "Today I think I will lie to my boss" or "This afternoon I think I will get hooked on internet pornography" or "Tonight I will sink into depression." Rather, he takes us down the delicate path of deception, an inch at a time.

That's the problem with deception. It's never recognized until it's too late. His tricks are timeless; his schemes subtle. To stand firm against his tactics, we must put on the first piece of essential armor.

VIDEO NOTES

Introduction: Guerrilla Warfare

1. Satan was _____ at the Cross.

2. Sin's _____ was paid for all people for all time.

3. Sin's _____ was broken.

4. Yet, Satan and his host of fallen angels engage in guerrilla warfare to *discourage, deceive, divide, and destroy* God's people and God's program.

5. Believers are commanded to _____ and _____ themselves in the strength of the Lord and in His mighty power to stand firm against the Enemy's schemes, repel his multi-faceted attacks, and engage and defeat him in specific battles. — *Ephesians 6:10-12*

How to Prepare Yourself for Satanic Attack

¹³Therefore, take up the full armor of God, that you may be able to resist in the evil day, and having done everything, to stand firm. ¹⁴Stand firm therefore, having girded your loins with truth, and having put on the breastplate of righteousness, ¹⁵and having shod your feet with the preparation of the gospel of peace;...

Ephesians 6:13—15 (NASB)

■ Our commander (Jesus Christ) _____ commands us to "pick up" our spiritual armor and put it on. *Verse 13*

Why? = For the purpose of being **fully prepared** and **enabled** to withstand the grave and difficult "dark times" when the Enemy attacks.

- After picking up our armor in preparation for battle, we are then commanded to _____ and **vigorously** make a _____ **act** (or succession of acts) to stand our ground firmly and fearlessly against the Enemy's assaults as he seeks to deceive, accuse, and discourage us. Verse 14a

"Having girded your loins with truth"

- Satan's first attack on mankind was _____ which was followed by man's hiding, denial, and blame shifting.

- Application:

Search me, O God, and know my heart; test me and know my anxious thoughts. See if there is any offensive way in me, and lead me in the way everlasting.

Psalm 139:23-24 (NASB)

DISCUSSION QUESTIONS

1. What new insight did you gain about the belt of truth from Chip's teaching today?

_____

_____

_____

2. Why is it so important to be totally honest with God, others, and ourselves in light of Satan's primary tactic to deceive us as believers?

_____

_____

_____

3. Share one specific instance (as is appropriate for this group) when you've been less than honest with God and yourself in the past. What were the implications of your failure to be honest? How did the Enemy use that destructively in your life?

_____

_____

_____

4. Share a time in the last month where you have been less than honest with a person. How does God want us to deal with those times (that we all experience as fallen human beings) when we fail to be honest with God or others? See 1 John 1:9 and Ephesians 4:15 and 25.

_____

_____

_____

5. It is often said that everyone wears a mask. In other words, insecurity drives us all to posture and pose in certain situations to make a good impression on others. How can the truth of our position in Christ help us take off our mask?

_____

_____

_____

Session 3 Keys

Satan's first and main tactic against us is to deceive, deceive, deceive.

The "belt of truth" is blatant honesty with others, our God, and ourselves.

The belt of truth is "the man or woman whose mind will practice no deceit and no disguises in their walk with God."

Kenneth Wuest

ACTION STEPS

Take Chip's challenge. Read Psalm 139:23–24:

> [23]*Search me, O God, and know my heart; try me and know my anxious thoughts;* [24]*and see if there be any hurtful way in me, and lead me in the everlasting way.*

Psalm 139:23—24 (NASB)

Pray through these words; ask the Lord:

- Where am I deceived?
- How's my heart?
- Have I hurt anyone?

When His search light pinpoints those hidden sins, confess them quickly. The loving, gracious, and holy God we serve does not hold grudges. Once you have made peace with God, if He brought anyone to your mind, make peace with them; the quicker, the better.

AT HOME

Satan's first attack on humanity has been his most proven and trusted one: deception. Satan twists the truth just enough to make sin justifiable, to keep holiness unattractive, and to point the finger at someone other than ourselves.

Chip listed a few commonly quoted lies from our present culture:

- Take care of yourself first and foremost
- The Bible was written centuries ago, it's not relevant today
- Truth is relative, what's true for you may not be true for me
- If God were all loving, He would never allow such bad things to happen
- I'm going to stand up for my rights, regardless of the consequences

What lies are you buying into? Because deception is so difficult to detect, this week have a conversation with a trusted friend about lies that you are prone to believe. Be honest and vulnerable. Ask them to tell you if they notice you slipping into Satan's subtle traps.

The Enemy's Attack:	Putting on the Armor:
Deceive	Belt of Truth: *Honesty with God*

MEMORY VERSES

Search me, O God, and know my heart; test me and know my anxious thoughts. See if there is any offensive way in me, and lead me in the way everlasting.

Psalms 139:23—24 (NASB)

HOW TO PREPARE YOURSELF FOR
SPIRITUAL
BATTLE

Ephesians 6:13—15

How To Prepare Yourself For Spiritual Battle

Guilt. There's good guilt. The kind that drives a repentant person to his knees. The guilt that says, "I'm sorry, please forgive me." Such guilt promotes grace.

Then there's the other kind.

The guilt that drives a person to legalism. The guilt prodded by accusations of "you're not good enough" or "you must earn My love."

The guilt that measures spirituality by external appearances. Such guilt paralyzes grace.

One is a tool of God, the other of Satan. One seeks grace, the other snatches grace. One feels like liberty, the other legalism. What's the difference? How do we become grace-promoters rather than grace-paralyzers?

VIDEO NOTES

How to Prepare Yourself for Satanic Attack (cont'd)

1. "Having girded your loins with truth"

2. "Having put on the breastplate of righteousness"

   - _____ = Uprightness, right living, integrity in one's lifestyle and character — conforming of our will to God's will.

   - Satan's attacks are not merely deception, but accusation (resulting in guilt and condemnation) of the believer. When we willfully turn away from what we know is God's will, we open ourselves to demonic influence in our lives.

   - Old Testament = Saul

   - New Testament = Peter

   - Application: "Therefore to the one who knows what is right to do and doesn't do it, to him it is sin." — *James 4:17 (NASB)*

     Personal area to address = _____

3. "Having shod your feet with the preparation of the gospel of peace"

   - _____ = Establishment — the means of a firm foundation; also conveys the idea of readiness to share the gospel which brings peace between man and God.

   - Satan not only uses _____ and _____ to neutralize believers, but also specializes in **casting doubt** on the very basis of God's goodness and the means by which we have received it — the gospel.

   - Application:

     1. **Know** and _____ the content of the gospel.
        1 Corinthians 15:1–5; Ephesians 2:1–9

     2. Know the basis for your _____ and the **assurance of your salvation**. Security — *Romans 8:38–39; Ephesians 1:13–14.* Assurance — *1 John 5:11–13*

     3. Faith is based on _____ , not feelings.

4. Sharing your faith is one of the most powerful faith-builders available. Often "the best defense is a good offense."

CONCLUSION

The spiritual battle we fight involves a responsibility on our part to "put on" the spiritual protection that God has provided for us. We can and will resist the Enemy's attempts to "deceive," "accuse," and "cast doubt" when we stand firm against him by:

1. Being honest with God, ourselves and others as a prerequisite to all spiritual battle.

2. Responding to the truth that God shows us about His will for our lives — righteous living.

3. Clearly understanding the gospel and the habitual sharing of this message of grace.

DISCUSSION QUESTIONS

1. What new insight did you gain about the "**Breastplate of Truth**" from this session's teaching? What vital organ does a physical breastplate protect, and what are the spiritual implications? *(See Proverbs 4:23)*

2. How are we to respond to "true guilt" when the Spirit of God has shown us there is a discrepancy between our belief and our behavior? *(See 1 John 1:9)* How are we to respond when Satan's condemnations or when "false guilt" is the source of our condemnation? *(See Romans 8:1)* How can you tell the difference between the conviction of the Holy Spirit and the condemnation of the Enemy?

3. Share a time in the last two weeks when the Spirit convicted you and you practiced 1 John 1:9. What were the results? Share as honestly and appropriately as possible so that we can learn from one other.

4. Why is it so important to understand your security in Christ? Is it possible for a believer to be fully assured of his or her salvation and know with certainty that we are going to heaven? Please read 1 John 5:11–13 out loud in the group. What promise is made in verse 13 to every genuine believer?

5. The security of our salvation is rooted in a clear understanding of the gospel of grace. From what you've learned in today's session, break off in pairs and take 5 minutes to practice clearly articulating the gospel. Remember, the gospel message always involves four specific components:

>   **1.** There is a problem — man's sin separates him from God. *(Romans 3:23)*
>
>   **2.** There is a solution — Christ's death on the cross paid for all the sin of all the men of all time, being fully God and fully man. *(Romans 5:8)*
>
>   **3.** God's solution (the payment price of Christ's blood for our sin) is a gift and can never be earned but needs to be received by faith. *(Ephesians 2:8–9)*
>
>   **4.** We need to personally receive God's gift of salvation by faith. *(John 1:12)*

Session 4 Keys

"Righteousness" is the practical application of God's truth.

The Enemy uses guilt to attack grace.

We must fight the "feelings" that try and shake the "facts" of our firm foundation.

Therefore there is now no condemnation for those who are in Christ Jesus.

Romans 8:1 (NASB)

ACTION STEPS

We usually measure our spiritual life with a predictable checklist of dos and don'ts.

When we reduce Christianity to a check list, we focus on external signs of spirituality rather than the internal. While prayer, bible study, and consistent giving are important to the Christian life, they mean nothing if we ignore the bitterness, anger, or jealousy rooting in our hearts.

1. Write out a personal area you are struggling with:

_____

_____

_____

2. Commit today to resolve the issue with God and anyone involved.

AT HOME

Jesus said that we can build our life upon a "firm foundation;" one that will stand strong through the emotional peaks and valleys of our life. To do this we must first ground ourselves in the **facts** of the gospel or we will forever be a slave to our **feelings**.

1. Gospel: Meditate on John 3:16; Romans 6:23; 1 Corinthians 15:1–5; Ephesians 2:1–9. Write out the **facts** of the gospel below. Pick one verse from this section to memorize this week.

_____

_____

_____

2. Security and Assurance: Meditate on John 10:28–29; Romans 8:38–39; Ephesians 1:13–14; 1 John 5:11–13. Write out the facts of our eternal security in Christ. Pick one verse from this section to memorize this week.

_____

_____

_____

The Enemy's Attack:	Putting on the Armor:
Deceive	**Belt of Truth:** *Honesty with God*
Accuse	**Breastplate of Righteousness:** *Apply what you know to be true*
Cast Doubt	**Shod *your* Feet:** *Understanding the gospel*

MEMORY VERSE

If we confess our sins, He is faithful and righteous to forgive us our sins and to cleanse us from all unrighteousness.

1 John 1:9 (NASB)

ENGAGING THE ENEMY

Ephesians 6:16–17

Engaging The Enemy

Up until this point our conversation on spiritual warfare has been relatively safe. Deception, accusations, doubt — nothing weird there. Those subtle schemes of the Enemy are all well documented and experienced by many believers. Sometimes you may have even encountered this disturbing evil.

What do you do when you experience the very disturbing direct attacks of the Enemy? Not just a subtle accusation or moments of doubt — but the palatable presence of evil? It may be rare, but it's real. When the dark clouds descend on you, how do you protect yourself?

VIDEO NOTES

How to do Battle with the Enemy and Win
Ephesians 6:16-17

I.   **Introduction: Four Facts You Need to Know**

FACT #1

God has objectively defeated Satan and his agenda. He has delivered us from sin's penalty and power and ultimately will deliver us from sin's very presence. In the interim, we are involved in guerrilla warfare with demonic forces.

FACT #2

As believers, we have been transferred from the kingdom of darkness to the Kingdom of light with all the rights, privileges, and position that being a child of God entails.

FACT #3

The spiritual battle we fight involves a responsibility on our part to "put on" the spiritual protection that God has provided for us. We can and will resist the Enemy's attempts to "deceive," "accuse," and "cast doubt" when we stand firm against him by:

1. Being honest with God, ourselves, and others as a prerequisite to all spiritual battle.

2. Responding to the truth that God shows us about His will for our lives — righteous living.

3. Understanding and readily sharing the "gospel message" of grace.

FACT #4

The great majority of spiritual warfare need never go beyond the regular practice of living out our position in Christ by faith. Our practice of Paul's metaphor of the spiritual armor protects us from Satan's ongoing attempts to break our fellowship with Jesus and, as a result, greatly minimizes any impact by the Enemy.

The Question:
Once you're wearing your spiritual armor and yet find yourself bombarded by spiritual opposition, How Do You Engage and Win the Battles?

The Answer:
Ephesians 6:16-17 (NASB)

> *"...in addition to all, taking up the shield of faith with which you will be able to extinguish all the flaming missiles of the evil one."* **Verse 16**

> *"And take the helmet of salvation, and the sword of the Spirit, which is the word of God."* **Verse 17**

II. **How to Engage the Enemy and Win — Ephesians 6:16-17**

  1. "Taking up the shield of faith" Verse 16

  - **Definition = Faith** in this context is our "absolute confidence" in God, His _____ , His power and His program for our lives.

  - Its purpose — to quench _____ the fiery missiles of the evil one.

  - **"Fiery darts/missiles"** = The schemes, temptations, lies, deceptions, and attacks aimed at (us) God's people to get us to "shift our focus" to something or someone other than God.

    These are often rooted in lies about God's identity or our new identity in Christ.

> *Do not love the world nor the things in the world. If anyone loves the world, the love of the Father is not in him. For all that is in the world, the lust of the flesh and the lust of the eyes and the boastful pride of life, is not from the Father, but is from the world.*
>
> *1 John 2:15—16 (NASB)*

- **Application** = Darts of doubt and deception must be immediately met by the shield of faith. (i.e. your active, present, application of truth to your personal situation as soon as you recognize a dart has been received). How?

  1. Trusting in God's Character

  2. Trusting in God's Promises and Word

  3. Trusting in God's Program and Timing

DISCUSSION QUESTIONS

1. After listening to today's teaching, have you ever had an experience that you believe was a frontal attack with demonic activity? If so, share briefly what occurred and when. *(Remember confidentiality is crucial to the health of any small group. We all experience things that we either do not understand or at times may embarrass us.)*

_____

_____

_____

2. What new insight did you gain about taking up the shield of faith when enemy attacks come? What is the specific role of knowing God's promises and His Word as you practice taking up the shield of faith?

_____

_____

_____

3. What specific promises of the four listed concerning our victory in Christ were most helpful to you and why?

_____

_____

_____

4. Which of those promises do you need to hide in your heart so that you can be ready to quench any and every fiery dart the Enemy would shoot your way?

_____

_____

_____

5. Share one specific situation that you need to apply faith to today. Ask the group to help you identify which of God's promises would be most helpful for you at this time. Take _a few moments_ to close this session by praying for one another in the area needed that was shared by each person.

_____

_____

_____

Session 5 Keys

Usually Satan bombards us when we are taking steps of spiritual growth.

The shield of faith is our absolute confidence in God and His promises for our life.

Our faith is a "present faith in the Lord Jesus for victory over sin and the host of demonic forces."

Kenneth Wuest

ACTION STEPS

Chip talked about how darts of doubt and deception must be immediately met by the shield of faith.

Write these questions with the verses on a little card. Keep it with you and claim those verses when you go through a "frontal assault." Immediately respond by trusting in the truth of God's Word.

1. Am I trusting in God's character?
God has my best in mind. *Psalm 84:11, Romans 8:32*

2. Am I trusting in God's promises and Word?
He will accomplish what concerns me. *Numbers 23:19, 2 Peter 1:2–4*

3. Am I trusting in God's program and timing?
His ways are not always easiest, but are always best. *Jeremiah 29:11, Isaiah 55:8–13*

AT HOME

Great generals win battles because they make a habit of studying their Enemy and his tactics. You do this by analyzing past battles. This week, check out these two passages of scripture and observe *when, where, and how* each person was tempted by our Enemy.

Genesis 3

Matthew 4:1–11

What consistencies do you find in these two passages?

How did Jesus respond differently than Adam and Eve?

How have you seen the Enemy use these tactics in your life?

The Enemy's Attack:	Putting on the Armor:
Deceive	**Belt of Truth:** Honesty with God
Accuse	**Breastplate of Righteousness:** Apply what you know to be true
Cast Doubt	**Shod your Feet:** Understanding the gospel
Fiery Darts of Temptations, Lies, Deceptions	**Shield of Faith:** Absolute confidence in God, His promises, His power, and His program for our lives

MEMORY VERSES

Do not love the world or the things in the world. If anyone loves the world, the love of the Father is not in him. For all that is in the world, the lust of the flesh and the lust of the eyes and the boastful pride of life, is not from the Father, but is from the world.

I John 2:15—16 (NASB)

WINNING THE WAR

Ephesians 6:16–17

Winning The War

Even the sounds of some words betray their meanings. Few words are as exciting as "scintillating", or as depressing as "gloomy", as powerful as "dynamite", or as dull as, well, "dull."

In short, dullness takes the sharpness out of life. For much of life, "dull" means some temporary discomfort. But in battle, a dull blade means certain death.

No warrior worth his salt would dare enter a skirmish without a sharp sword. Yet, on a daily basis, Christians step onto the spiritual battlefield with little more than a butter knife.

In this session we are going to learn how to do hand-to-hand combat with the Enemy.

VIDEO NOTES

How to do Battle with the Enemy and Win
Ephesians 6:16-17

1. "Taking up the shield of faith" *Verse 16*

2. "And take the helmet of salvation" *Verse 17*

   - **Definition** = 1) Obvious allusion to the security we have as saved, justified believers, safe from Satan's attacks. But, focus is on present deliverance from sin! 2) The helmet of salvation is the certainty of deliverance from sin and the protection of our minds in the battle.

   - How? Focus is God's renewing of the believer's mind. *Romans 12:2, Romans 8:5–8* — ***2 Corinthians 10:5* = The battle is for the mind!**

   - Practically — Prayer, worship, music, scripture, teaching, scripture memory, fellowship

3. "And take...the sword of the Spirit" Verse 17

   - **Definition** = The sword of the Spirit is the Word (rhema — spoken word, or words given to us by the Spirit of God) to do close, hand-to-hand combat with the lies and deceptions of the Enemy.

   - **Example** — Jesus models for us the use of the sword of the Spirit. *Matthew 4:1–11*

   - Implications for us. *Psalm 119:105, Psalm 19:9, 11*

   - Practical considerations — Note that the sword is both a **defensive** and an **offensive** weapon. *Hebrews 4:12*

SUMMARY

How to Engage the Enemy in Spiritual Warfare

1. Prerequisite is a healthy spiritual life

2. Understand your position in Christ

3. Discern when demonic influence may be the cause

4. Claim God's promises out loud. *1 John 4:4, 1 John 5:4-5*

5. Take our authority and position in Christ to command demonic forces to cease their activity and depart.

KEY RESOURCES

Biblical Text

> James 4:1-8
>
> Ephesians 6:11-18
>
> 1 John 4:4, 5:4-5
>
> Revelation 12:10-12

Books = Balanced Reading

> *The Invisible War* — Donald Grey Barnhouse
>
> *Spiritual Warfare* — Ray C. Stedman
>
> *The Adversary* — Mark Bubeck
>
> *Overcoming the Adversary* — Mark Bubeck

DISCUSSION QUESTIONS

1. Share some specific ways that you've learned over the years to renew your mind (i.e. What you do in your devotional time, scripture memory, times of worship, great books, etc.). Share with the group some very specific ways that have helped you put on the helmet of salvation.

2. Share with the group some specific ways that you guard your mind from evil. For example — are there movies, TV shows, books, or certain types or content of music that you do not allow to go into your mind? Share your personal convictions about what you allow into your mind and why.

_____

_____

_____

3. What is your specific game plan to renew your mind with God's Word? Read Psalm 119: 9 and 11, and explain how this passage relates to the sword of the Spirit.

_____

_____

_____

4. From Jesus' example, in Matthew 4:1–11, why is it so important that we have key passages of scripture memorized so that we can not merely know them, but actually "speak them out loud" when confronting the Enemy?

_____

_____

_____

5. What specific passages have been most helpful to you in any spiritual battles that you've encountered in the past?

_____

_____

_____

Session 6 Keys

Salvation means that we are free from sin's power over our lives.

We attack Satan's lies with the truth from Scripture.

ACTION STEPS

No soldier would enter a battle with a dull sword.

Sharpen your sword by starting a scripture memory plan, even if it's one verse a week. Write them down on index cards, review them in the car, while you're riding the bus, or waiting to pick up the kids.

Take the verses in this guide and write them down and commit them to memory.

AT HOME

Let's look back and summarize how to engage the Enemy in spiritual warfare. As you review these points, write down how well you're doing with each principle:

1. Maintain a healthy spiritual life

_____

_____

_____

2. Understand your position in Christ, that you are a favored child of God

_____

_____

_____

3. Discern when demonic activity is the cause of your struggle

4. Claim God's promises out loud

5. Use your authority and position in Christ to command demonic forces to cease their activity and depart.

The Enemy's Attack:	Putting on the Armor:
Deceive	**Belt of Truth:** *Honesty with God*
Accuse	**Breastplate of Righteousness:** *Apply what you know to be true*
Cast Doubt	**Shod *your Feet:*** *Understanding the gospel*
Fiery Darts of Temptations, Lies, Deceptions	**Shield of Faith:** *Absolute confidence in God, His promises, His power, and His program for our lives*
Battle for our Minds	**Helmet of Salvation:** *Certainty that we are delivered from sin*
Hand-to-Hand Combat	**Sword of the Spirit:** *Knowing God's Word*

MEMORY VERSE

For whatever is born of God overcomes the world; and this is the victory that has overcome the world — our faith. Who is the one who overcomes the world, but he who believes that Jesus is the Son of God?

1 John 5:4—5 (NASB)

THE CHRISTIAN'S SECRET WEAPON

Ephesians 6:18—20

The Christian's Secret Weapon

David cried out to the Lord, *"But I, O Lord, have cried out to You for help, and in the morning my prayer comes before You."* Nehemiah spent three months in prayer before presenting his plan of rebuilding the walls to King Artaxerxes. Jesus journeyed to the mountains for times of prayer. Paul said, *"pray without ceasing."* In the Bible, prayer is treated as necessary, never optional.

But if we're honest, prayer remains a missing ingredient in our spiritual lives.

In this session, Chip will talk to us about how such an absence will produce a powerless life. We will learn why intercessory prayer is our most powerful weapon in this cosmic conflict.

VIDEO NOTES

How to Gain Deliverance from Demonic Influence

Introduction: The "Missing Ingredient"

Ephesians 6:10–12 (NASB)   >   **We are in an invisible war.**

Ephesians 6:13–15 (NASB)   >   **We are to prepare ourselves for battle.**

Ephesians 6:16–17 (NASB)   >   **When we resist the Enemy, he will flee from us.**

18With all prayer and petition pray at all times in the Spirit, and with this in view, be on the alert with all perseverance and petition for all the saints, 19and pray on my behalf, that utterance may be given to me in the opening of my mouth, to make known with boldness the mystery of the gospel, 20for which I am an ambassador in chains; that in proclaiming it I may speak boldly, as I ought to speak.

>   **Intercessory prayer is pivotal and essential for corporate and individual deliverance.**

Ephesians 6:18—20 (NASB)

Summary of *Ephesians 6:18–20* — The means by which believers are to withstand and overcome the attacks of the Enemy in spiritual warfare is by consistent, intense, strategic prayer for one another in conjunction with the personal application of the armor of God.

I.   Intercessory prayer is our most powerful and strategic corporate weapon in spiritual warfare.

- Prayer has a direct impact on spiritual warfare. *Mark 9:29*

- Prayer provides/assists in the deliverance of others who are undergoing spiritual attack. *Luke 22:31–32*

- Power falls where prayer prevails. *Acts 1:14, 2:42, 3:1, 4:24–35, 6:4–8, 8:14–16, 9:40–42, 10:1–4*, Church history is replete with examples.

II.   What kind of prayer brings God's deliverance and power in the midst of spiritual attack?

- _____ **Prayer** *Verse 18a*

- "with all prayer and petition" = all kinds of prayer

- "pray at all times" = prayer on all occasions

- "pray in the spirit" = in communion with and directed by the agency and power of the Holy Spirit

- _____ **Prayer** *Verse 18b*

- "be on the alert" = lit. = without sleep, vigilant

- "with all perseverance" = enduring, not giving up

- _____ **Prayer** *Verse 18c–20*

- "for all the saints" = that God's messengers will be bold

- "utterance may be given" = God's message will be clear and have opportunity

Summary = The _____ _____ in most Christians' lives and in most churches is the commitment and regular practice of intercessory prayer. Scripture indicates that (individual and corporate) consistent, intense, and strategic intercessory prayer will in fact "deliver us from the evil one."

THE CHRISTIAN'S SECRET WEAPON   7

"The great people of the earth today are the people who pray. I do not mean those who talk about prayer; nor those who say they believe in prayer; nor yet those who can explain about prayer; but I mean those people who take time and pray. They have not time. It must be taken from something else. This something else is important. Very important, and pressing, but still less important and less pressing than prayer."

S. D. Gordon

DISCUSSION QUESTIONS

1. Share briefly an experience where you saw how God answered specific prayers in a way that had dramatic impact in others lives. *(Ephesians 6:18–20)*

2. Are there some issues, roadblocks, or major concerns in your life currently being thwarted because you have not combated them with intense, consistent, and strategic intercessory prayer? If so, stop and have the group pray for you right now.

3. We learned in this session that it's not just "any kind of prayer" that brings results. What kind of prayer brings powerful results in spiritual warfare? List the three characteristics of this kind of prayer and share how you believe God wants these played out in our lives.

_____

_____

_____

4. Read S.D. Gordon's quote out loud in your group and share your reactions to it. Then on a scale of 1–10 (1 being weak, 10 being very strong), how would you rank your personal prayer life?

_____

_____

_____

5. What specific steps do you need to take to lay hold of this secret power of intercessory prayers available to every Christian? What would it look like for you to develop a more consistent prayer life? Who do you know that could help you learn to pray more intensely and strategically?

_____

_____

_____

Session 7 Keys

Power falls where prayer prevails.

Effective prayer takes consistency, intensity, and strategy.

Pray when you feel like praying. Pray when you don't feel like praying. Pray until you feel like praying.

Anonymous

ACTION STEPS

How are you doing in the three areas of intercessory prayer? Confess to God where you have fallen short. Then renew your commitment in a practical way. In the space below, write out one way you will improve each category of prayer:

1. **Consistent Prayer**

_____

_____

_____

2. **Intense Prayer**

_____

_____

_____

3. Strategic Prayer

_____

_____

_____

AT HOME

If prayer is the missing ingredient in a believer's life, then fasting has become a lost food group. Yet over and over in scripture we see Christians called to practice the discipline of fasting. This week, challenge yourself to fast a day or even just one meal and feast on God's spiritual food.

During that time, practice the ACTS method of prayer as you see below. With each step, write down your prayers. Let it be a model for future extended times of prayer.

1. Adoration

_____

_____

_____

2. Confession

_____

_____

_____

3. Thanksgiving

_____

_____

4. Supplication

_____

_____

_____

MEMORY VERSE

Be anxious for nothing, but in everything by prayer and supplication with thanksgiving let your requests be made known to God.

Philippians 4:6 (NASB)

THE MINISTRY OF DELIVERANCE

Ephesians 6:18–20

The Mystery Of Deliverance

There's just something special about graduation day. There's something about putting on the black gown, donning the cardboard hat, turning the tassel, and grabbing the diploma.

It speaks of finality, completion, and closure. But on another level, it's a beginning — a start, the trailhead to a new adventure.

In this session, we will wrap up our study on spiritual warfare.

God's desire is that we graduate as changed people: ready for the adventure and prepared for the battle.

VIDEO NOTES

How to Gain Deliverance from Demonic Influence

III. The Ministry of Deliverance

    A. Its Validity

- Jesus regularly exercised this ministry. *(Mark 1:27, 39)*
- The apostles regularly exercised this ministry. *(Luke 10)*
- The early church regularly exercised this ministry. *(Acts 16)*
- Athanasius *(c. 296–373)*
- The New Testament writers provide clear direction concerning this ministry. *(James 4:1–10)*
- Contemporary, balanced deliverance ministries do exist and help many people.

    B. Its Problems

- Extremism and fanaticism tend to negatively color this ministry.
- Confusion concerning demon possession versus oppression of believers clouds this ministry's validity among Christians.
- Fear and ignorance have caused many to simply ignore this ministry.
- Those who engage in this ministry are often tempted by pride or become so singularly focused they fall into theological error.
- Assigning blame of all one's problems to demonic influence versus assuming personal responsibility and using Biblical common sense call this ministry into question.

    C. The Cause(s) of Demonic Influence

- Yielding to sin *(John 8:34)*
- Spiritual rebellion *(1 Samuel 15:23)*
- Participating in the occult *(Deuteronomy 18:10–11)*
- Attempting to contact the dead *(Deuteronomy 18:11)*

- ■ Unresolved anger and bitterness *(Ephesians 4:26–27)*

- ■ Association with those involved in Satanic activity
  (2 Corinthians 6:14–16)

D. New Testament Evidences of Demonic Influence

- ■ Severe sickness *(Matthew 12:22)*

- ■ Divination — telling the future *(Acts 16:16)*

- ■ Unusual physical strength *(Mark 5:3)*

- ■ Fits of rage *(Mark 5:4)*

- ■ Split personality *(Mark 5:6–7)*

- ■ Resistance to spiritual help *(Mark 5:7)*

- ■ Other voices from within *(Mark 5:9)*

- ■ Occult powers *(Deuteronomy 18:10–11)*

E. The Cure for Demonic Influence
General Purpose

1. Victory is through the cross of Christ (Colossians 2:14–15)

2. Victory is in the name of Christ (Matthew 10:1, Acts 5:16)

3. Victory is in the power of the Holy Spirit (1 John 4:4)

Specific Steps for Deliverance from Demonic Influence

1. Accept Christ *(John 1:12)*

2. Confess sins *(1 John 1:9)*

3. Renounce works of the devil *(2 Corinthians 4:2)*

4. Destroy occult objects *(Acts 19:17–20;
see also 2 Chronicles 14:2, 23:17)*

5. Break friendship with occultists *(2 Corinthians 6:14–16)*

6. Rest in Christ's deliverance *(Colossians 1:13)*

7. Resist the devil *(James 4:7–10)*

8. Meditate on and apply the Word of God *(Ephesians 6:17,
Matthew 4:4, 7, 10)*

9. Engage in corporate prayer (Ephesians 6:18, Matthew 18:19)

10. If necessary, exorcism in the name of Christ (Acts 16:16)

    a. By a spiritually qualified counselor (Galatians 5:16, Ephesians 5:18)

- Who maintains humility (James 4:7)

- Who wears spiritual armor (Ephesians 6:12f)

- Who knows the Word of God (Matthew 4:4, 7, 10)

- Who is supported by prayers of believers (Ephesians 6:18, Matthew 18:19)

F. Additional Resources For Help When You Suspect Demonic Influence

The Adversary — Mark I. Bubeck

Overcoming The Adversary — Mark I. Bubeck

Powers of Evil — A Biblical Study of Satan & Demons — Sydney H.T. Page

DISCUSSION QUESTIONS

1. Why do you think the topic of deliverance ministry is so controversial? What extremes have caused you to question genuine deliverance ministry as being real and biblical?

2. In what specific ways do we open ourselves up to demonic involvement? Of the six ways listed in your notes, where are you most prone or likely to knowingly or unknowingly open yourself to demonic activity?

3. Is there any person or situation that from what you've learned so far causes you to suspect ongoing demonic activity that may be in need of deliverance? If so, what pastor or spiritual leader can you contact about beginning to address the situation?

4. Why is bitterness or anger such a pathway for the devil in the life of a believer?

5. Of the ten steps Chip listed for deliverance, which one(s) do you need to apply today to your life?

Session 8 Keys

We need to view demonic influence with a balanced approach.

There are specific steps every believer can take to be delivered from demonic influence.

Prayer is not monologue, but dialogue; God's voice is its most essential part. Listening to God's voice is the secret of the assurance that He will listen to mine.

Andrew Murray

ACTION STEPS

Chip asked the question, "Where do you go from here?" It's so easy to complete a great study, have some great emotional and spiritual experiences, and shelve the workbook forever. In order for knowledge to stick, we have to apply what we've learned. Take some time to read Psalm 84:11:

For the Lord God is a sun and shield; The Lord gives grace and glory; No good thing does He withhold from those who walk uprightly.

Psalm 84:11

1. Now, in light of all you have gained, what is the one thing God wants you to do in His grace? Write it down and make that your ambition as you prepare to close this study.

AT HOME

Let's get practical for a moment. Chip mentioned a few things that we can do to meditate on and apply the Word of God to our lives. As we end this study, make a commitment to start something new in your spiritual life. May you leave this study different than when you began it — for Christianity is about growth, not stagnation.

Meditation involves time, commitment, and intentionality. Below are a few ideas that could help you in your application of God's Word. Pick one, or think of another, and then commit before God that you will follow through.

Ideas:

- **Media fast** — Take at least a ten day break from all media. Use that time to read and meditate on God's Word.

- **Read through the *New Testament* in three weeks** — We do it with novels, why not the eternal wisdom of God?

- **Memory program** — You have plenty of verses within this study to start a Bible memorization program. Let the Word be written on your heart.

On this day, _____ ,

I, _____ ,

(NAME)

commit to meditate and apply God's Word to my life by

_____ _____.

I trust that God will illuminate His wisdom to me
through the power of His Spirit.

_____
SIGNATURE

MEMORY VERSE

For He rescued us from the domain of darkness, and transferred us to the kingdom of His beloved Son.

Colossians 1:13 (NASB)

LEADING YOUR GROUP THROUGH
THE INVISIBLE
WAR

THE TOOLS FOR THIS SERIES

This course has been developed to bring the principles of this series alive in each participant's life. Thank you for your willingness to lead this study.

The Invisible War is intended to be more than just a study. It is an 8-week experience that will equip the people in your group to do spiritual battle with the Enemy of their soul and win. It contains eight video sessions featuring the teaching of Chip Ingram.

The Study Guide is designed to help each participant personalize the lessons. It contains: **Video Notes** complete with a fill-in-the-blank outline for taking notes during each of the video sessions; penetrating **group discussion questions** that correspond with each lesson; and life-changing **exercises** to implement the lessons into everyday life.

To order extra materials for *The Invisible War*, call Living on the Edge at **1-888-333-6003** or log on at ***www.LivingontheEdge.org***

GETTING STARTED – 4 EASY STEPS

Several basic ingredients are essential to any successful group study. Before you plan the first meeting, you should work through these fundamentals.

1. **First, pray!** Only God can change the hearts of men, and prayer is your most powerful tool. As the leader of your group, this is your logical starting place.

2. **Next, organize.** Consider asking one or two others to share the leadership load by helping you plan, promote the series, distribute materials, etc.

3. **Order the Study Guides.** Before starting the course, make sure that each participant has his own copy of the Study Guide. This series is designed to be highly interactive, and the Study Guide is essential for integrating the principles into daily life.

4. **Prepare to lead the sessions.** Pray and get prepared for each week. Your preparation will make a big difference in the group's experience.

THINGS TO REMEMBER WHILE LEADING THIS SERIES

Tried and True Tips for the Successful Video Series Leader

Create a Friendly Environment: Remember it's not about the material, it's about the people.

Focus on Facilitating, Not Teaching: For nearly thirty years Chip has been studying scripture, counseling, and exploring the issues surrounding spiritual warfare. Since he brings his expertise to every session, that means you can sit back and relax while he presents the material. Your expertise is needed in facilitating his teaching and cultivating good conversation during the discussion time.

Be Yourself: The others in your group will appreciate and follow your example of openness and honesty as you lead — so set a good example! The best way to encourage those in your class is not to impress them with your own wisdom, but with your sincere desire to live out these principles in your own life. When they sense that you are "real" — that you are not "above" the issues that challenge them — they will be encouraged to press on. The transparency of your group may be the crucial ingredient that sparks their motivation.

Be Prepared: Hopefully, the discussion questions will raise some interesting conversation in your group. However, you can also lose focus during discussion time as people present opinions that may detract from the focus of the lesson, or may not represent Biblical teaching. A good way to keep things on track is to point the conversation back to the material. We recommend that you view each video session before your group arrives.

ABOUT YOUR VIDEO TEACHER

Chip Ingram's passion is to help Christians really live like Christians. As a pastor, author, coach, and teacher for twenty-five years, Chip has helped people around the world break out of spiritual ruts to live out God's purpose for their lives. Today, he serves as senior pastor of Venture Christian Church in Los Gatos, California, and president of Living on the Edge – an international teaching and discipleship ministry. He is the author of eleven books, including *Overcoming Emotions That Destroy* and *Good to Great in God's Eyes*. Chip and his wife, Theresa, have four children and eight grandchildren..

HOW TO STRUCTURE YOUR GROUP TIME

Whether you are leading this series in a home or a classroom, you'll find the materials are ideal for most small group settings. The course is designed so that the video teaching and the discussion questions will fit into one hour segments. Of course, you can take extra time for discussion or to review the previous week's material if time permits.

Below is the suggested way to use these materials.

IN CLASS

1. **Video Class Notes:** Each video session has a corresponding section in the Study Guide for participants to follow along as Chip teaches. A fill-in-the-blank outline highlights the main points of the video, and there is room for additional notes and insights as well. The "answers" to the notes can be found in the Leader's Guide for each session.

2. **Discussion Questions:** The Study Guide also contains discussion questions for each of the video sessions. They are designed to help your participants personalize the content of each lesson. You can move to these questions immediately after the conclusion of the video.

   The main goal of these questions is to help you stir up discussion in your group. Encourage your group to answer with more than short "yes" and "no" answers. Use the questions to draw people into discussing their hearts, their struggles, and how the teaching could be applied to their personal situations.

3. **Action Steps:** The Study Guide then moves into specific action steps that are designed to help create specific ways to apply the material. Your group will benefit tremendously by sharing ideas and discussing the recommended action steps together. Make your group a safe environment for sharing personal struggles. Together, your group can minister to each other, helping to apply God's Word to everyday situations.

AFTER CLASS

4. **At Home:** These personal studies are intended to take the principles right off the page and into the lives of each student. As the participants immerse themselves in these materials each day, the transformation process begins. Encourage the people in your group to complete their assignments weekly.

SUGGESTED FORMAT

1. View the Video Lesson, filling in the notes in the Study Guide (25–35 minutes)

2. Discussion Questions (20 minutes)

3. Assignment for upcoming week (5 minutes)

4. Prayer requests, group prayer (10 minutes)

SESSION 1 — What is the Invisible War?

VIDEO NOTES

ANSWER KEY

I. _____GENERAL_____ **Command** *Verse 10*

II. _____SPECIFIC_____ **Command** *Verse 11*

III. The _____REASON_____ **for Commands in Verses 10–11** *Verse 12*

1. There is an invisible world that is just as _____REAL_____ as the Visible World. — *Ephesians 6:12*

2. We are involved in an _____INVISIBLE_____ war, a cosmic conflict that has eternal implications. — *Ephesians 6:12*

SESSION 2 — Who Are We Fighting?

VIDEO NOTES

ANSWER KEY

3. Our foe is _____FORMIDABLE_____ and His goal is to destroy us and discredit the cause of Christ. — *Ephesians 6:12*

4. We must respect our foe, but not fear him — become acutely _____AWARE_____ of his "methods," but not be preoccupied by them. — *Ephesians 6:11*

Satan's names reveal his _____SCHEMES_____ .

Satan attacks _____GOD'S_____ _____PROGRAM_____ , the church, by...

Satan attacks _____GOD'S_____ _____PEOPLE_____ by...

Satan's power is _____LIMITED_____ .

Session Notes

SESSION 3 — Four Keys to Spiritual Victory
VIDEO NOTES

ANSWER KEY

1. Satan was _____DEFEATED_____ at the Cross.

2. Sin's _____PENALTY_____ was paid for all people for all time.

3. Sin's _____POWER_____ was broken.

4. Yet, Satan and his host of fallen angels engage in guerrilla warfare to *discourage, deceive, divide, and destroy* God's people and God's program.

5. Believers are commanded to _____PREPARE_____ and _____EQUIP_____ themselves in the strength of the Lord and in His mighty power to stand firm against the Enemy's schemes, repel his multi-faceted attacks, and engage and defeat him in specific battles. — *Ephesians 6:10-12*

■ Our commander (Jesus Christ) _____URGENTLY_____ commands us to "pick up" our spiritual armor and put it on. *Verse 13*

■ After picking up our armor in preparation for battle, we are then commanded to _____CONSISTENTLY_____ and **vigorously** make a _____DECISIVE_____ **act** (or succession of acts) to stand our ground firmly and fearlessly against the Enemy's assaults as he seeks to deceive, accuse, and discourage us. Verse 14a

"Having girded your loins with truth"

■ Satan's first attack on mankind was _____DECEPTION_____ which was followed by man's hiding, denial, and blame shifting.

SESSION 4 — How to Prepare Yourself for Spiritual Battle

VIDEO NOTES

ANSWER KEY

- ___RIGHTEOUSNESS___ = Uprightness, right living, integrity in one's lifestyle and character — conforming of our will to God's will. Although rooted in the object righteousness that we already possess in our standing before God through the work of Christ, this breastplate of righteousness (that guards and protects our heart) is the practical application of the truth to our lives — i.e. Lordship of Christ.

- ___PREPARATION___ = Establishment — the means of a firm foundation; also conveys the idea of readiness to share the gospel which brings peace between man and God.

- Satan not only uses ___DECEPTION___ and ___CONDEMNATION___ to neutralize believers, but also specializes in **casting doubt** on the very basis of God's goodness and the means by which we have received it — the gospel.

- Application:

  1. **Know** and ___UNDERSTAND___ the content of the gospel. *1 Corinthians 15:1–5; Ephesians 2:1–9*

  2. Know the basis for your ___ETERNAL SECURITY___ and the **assurance of your salvation**. Security — *Romans 8:38–39; Ephesians 1:13–14*. Assurance — *1 John 5:11–13*

  3. Faith is based on ___FACTS___ , not feelings.

ACTION STEPS

This exercise is helpful in revealing if the Enemy is using guilt to attack grace. When we reduce Christianity to a checklist, we focus on external signs of spirituality rather than the internal. While prayer, bible study, and consistent giving are important to the Christian life, they mean nothing if we ignore the bitterness, anger, or jealousy rooting in our hearts. Direct the group to write out a personal area they are struggling with and then share that with their accountability partner for continued prayer.

AT HOME

Renewal or renovation of the mind is crucial in any spiritual battle. This exercise will prompt the group to examine their personal foundation of faith and challenge them to memorize key scripture. At the next meeting see if anyone wants to volunteer and site the scripture they chose to memorize.

SESSION 5 — Engaging the Enemy
VIDEO NOTES

ANSWER KEY

1. "Taking up the shield of faith" Verse 16

   ■ **Definition = Faith** in this context is our "absolute confidence" in God, His _____PROMISES_____ , His power and His program for our lives.

   ■ Its purpose — to quench _____ALL_____ the fiery missiles of the evil one.

SESSION 6 — Winning the War
VIDEO NOTES

ANSWER KEY

There are no fill-ins for session 6.

SESSION 7 — The Christian's Secret Weapon
VIDEO NOTES

ANSWER KEY

- _____CONSISTENT_____ **Prayer** *Verse 18a*
- "with all prayer and petition" = all kinds of prayer
- _____INTENSE_____ **Prayer** *Verse 18b*
- _____STRATEGIC_____ **Prayer** *Verse 18c–20*

NOTES FOR DISCUSSION QUESTIONS

1. Share briefly an experience where you saw how God answered specific prayers in a way that had dramatic impact in others lives. How important is intercessory prayer with regard to experiencing victory in spiritual warfare according to this passage in today's teaching? (Ephesians 6:18–20)

This question is designed to invite discussion about the transforming power prayer can have in our lives. Sometimes it involves sitting back and listening to others share how God has worked in their lives through answered prayer.

2. Have you considered that some issues, roadblocks, or major concerns in your life are currently being thwarted because you have not combated them with intense, consistent, and strategic intercessory prayer?

This can be a compelling question and is intended to stir conversations among the participants in your group about intercessory prayer.

3. We learned in this session that it's not just "any kind of prayer" that brings results. What kind of prayer brings powerful results in spiritual warfare? List the three characteristics of this kind of prayer and share how you believe God wants these played out in our lives.

This question should generate discussion about the three types of prayer Chip discusses and how to use intercessory prayer as an active weapon in spiritual battle.

4. Read S.D. Gordon's quote out loud in your group and share your reactions to it. Then on a scale of 1–10 (1 being weak, 10 being very strong), how would you rank your personal prayer life?

There are no right or wrong answers here. The purpose of this question is to expose the crucial role that prayer plays in our lives.

5. What specific steps do you need to take to lay hold of this secret power of intercessory prayers available to every Christian? What would it look like for you to develop a more consistent prayer life? Who do you know that could help you learn to pray more intensely and strategically?

Throughout this series, it has been important to develop a personal vision for combating spiritual warfare. This question is designed to get everyone personally engaged in the war.

ACTION STEPS

Prayer is our secret weapon and certainly a necessity when at battle with the Enemy. How are you doing in the three areas of intercessory prayer? This action step is intended to help each participate renew their commitment to consistent, intense, and strategic prayer in a practical way.

AT HOME

If prayer is the missing ingredient in a believer's life, then fasting has become a lost food group. This exercise will help participants declare specific ways they can actively engage in consistent, intense, and strategic prayer through the ACTS method. (ACTS is only a guideline, feel free to use a prayer method that fits your groups style or need.)

SESSION 8 — *The Ministry of Deliverance*

VIDEO NOTES

ANSWER KEY

There are no fill-ins for session 8.

NOTES FOR DISCUSSION QUESTIONS

1. Why do you think the topic of deliverance ministry is so controversial? What extremes have caused you to question genuine deliverance ministry as being real and biblical?

This question will stir conversation among participants in your group and invite them to identify specifically which extremes have tainted their view of genuine deliverance ministry, as real and biblical.

2. In what specific ways do we open ourselves up to demonic involvement? Of the six ways listed in your notes, where are you most prone or likely to knowingly or unknowingly open yourself to demonic activity?

This question will help your group members honestly examine areas in which they are prone to the attack of demonic activity. By recognizing their areas of weakness, they can be better prepared with their shield of faith.

3. Is there any person or situation that from what you've learned so far causes you to suspect ongoing demonic activity that may be in need of deliverance? If so, what pastor or spiritual leader can you contact about beginning to address the situation?

This question provides a hands-on approach to what participants are learning about demonic activity. They do this by identifying where they see signs of demonic activity in their personal relationships. It also highlights the importance of contacting a spiritual leader in addressing the situation.

Session Notes

4. Why is bitterness or anger such a pathway for the devil in the life of a believer?

The purpose of this question is to expose the reasons why bitterness and anger give the devil power and a pathway into our lives as believers. This may help participants recognize the danger in harboring these qualities.

5. Of the ten steps Chip listed for deliverance, which one(s) do you need to apply today to your life?

Encouraging participants to choose and apply specific steps for deliverance will provide them with goals and motivation to take action.

ACTION STEPS

In order for knowledge to stick, we have to apply what we've learned. Have participants read Psalm 84:11 (provided in your workbook) and write down what God wants each of you to do in His grace. (examples provided in your workbook). Make that your ambition as you close this study.

AT HOME

Christianity is about growth, not stagnation. Encourage your group to make a commitment to start something new in their spiritual lives. The workbook mentions a few ideas that may help participants apply God's Word. As a group, each of you can pick one of these ideas, or think of another, and then commit before God that you will follow through.

What's Next?
More Group Studies from Chip Ingram:

Balancing Life's Demands
Biblical Priorities for a Busy Life

Busy, tired and stressed out? Learn how to put "first things first" and find peace in the midst of pressure and adversity.

BIO
How to Become An Authentic Disciple of Jesus

Unlock the Biblical DNA for spiritual momentum by examining the questions at the heart of true spirituality.

Culture Shock
A Biblical Response to Today's Most Divisive Issues

Bring light—not heat—to divisive issues, such as abortion, homosexuality, sex, politics, the environment, politics and more.

Doing Good
What Happens When Christians Really Live Like Christians

This series clarifies what Doing Good will do in you and then through you, for the benefit of others and the glory of God.

Effective Parenting in a Defective World
Raising Kids that Stand Out from the Crowd

Packed with examples and advice for raising kids, this series presents Biblical principles for parenting that still work today.

Experiencing God's Dream for Your Marriage
Practical Tools for a Thriving Marriage

Examine God's design for marriage and the real life tools and practices that will transform it for a lifetime.

Five Lies that Ruin Relationships
Building Truth-Based Relationships

Uncover five powerful lies that wreck relationships and experience the freedom of understanding how to recognize God's truth.

Watch previews and order at livingontheedge.org or 888.333.6003.

The Genius of Generosity
Lessons from a Secret Pact Between Friends
The smartest financial move you can make is to invest in God's Kingdom. Learn His design for wise giving and generous living.

God As He Longs for You to See Him
Seeing God With 20/20 Vision
A deeper look at seven attributes of God's character that will change the way you think, pray and live.

Good to Great in God's Eyes
10 Practices Great Christians Have in Common
If you long for spiritual breakthrough, take a closer look at ten powerful practices that will rekindle a fresh infusion of faith.

Heaven
It's Not What You Think
Chip Ingram digs into scripture to reveal what heaven will be like, what we'll do there, and how we're to prepare for eternity today.

Holy Ambition
Turning God-Shaped Dreams Into Reality
Do you long to turn a God-inspired dream into reality? Learn how God uses everyday believers to accomplish extraordinary things.

House or Home: Marriage Edition
God's Blueprint for a Great Marriage
Get back to the blueprint and examine God's plan for marriages that last for a lifetime.

House or Home: Parenting Edition
God's Blueprint for Biblical Parenting
Timeless truths about God's blueprint for parenting, and the potential to forever change the trajectory of your family.

Watch previews and order at livingontheedge.org or 888.333.6003.

The Invisible War
The Believer's Guide to Satan, Demons and Spiritual Warfare
Learn how to clothe yourself with God's "spiritual armor" and be confident of victory over the enemy of your soul.

Overcoming Emotions that Destroy
Constructive Tools for Destructive Emotions
We all struggle with destructive emotions that can ruin relationships. Learn God's plan to overcome angry feelings for good.

Rebuilding Your Broken World
How God Puts Broken Lives Back Together
Learn how God can reshape your response to trials and bring healing to broken relationships and difficult circumstances.

Spiritual Simplicity
Doing Less • Loving More
If you crave simplicity and yearn for peace this study is for you. Spiritual simplicity can only occur when we do less and love more.

Transformed
The Miracle of Life Change
Ready to make a change? Explore God's process of true transformation and learn to spot barriers that hold you back from receiving God's best.

True Spirituality
Becoming a Romans 12 Christian
We live in a world that is activity-heavy and relationship-light. Learn the next steps toward True Spirituality.

Why I Believe
Answers to Life's Most Difficult Question
Can miracles be explained? Is there really a God? There are solid, logical answers about claims of the Christian faith.

Your Divine Design
Discover, Develop and Deploy Your Spiritual Gifts
How has God uniquely wired you? Discover God's purpose

Watch previews and order at livingontheedge.org or 888.333.6003.